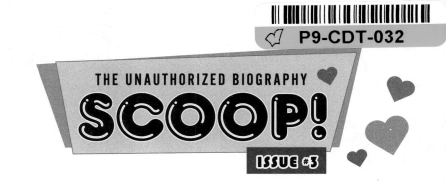

THE UNAUTHORIZED BIOGRAPHY
SCOOP!
ISSUE #3

Cast of Riverdale

by C. H. Mitford

Grosset & Dunlap

GROSSET & DUNLAP
An Imprint of Penguin Random House LLC, New York

Illustrations by Becky James

Photo credit: cover: Vivien Killilea/Stringer/Getty Images Entertainment/ Getty Images North America

Visit us online at www.penguinrandomhouse.com.

ISBN 9780593222270   10 9 8 7 6 5 4 3 2 1

TABLE OF CONTENTS

· ·

CHAPTER 1

NOT YOUR GRANDPA'S *RIVERDALE*

*A*re you binge-watching *Riverdale*? Because we are DEF binge-watching *Riverdale*. This show is straight-up addictive and pushing the boundaries of what we usually think of as "teen viewing." It can get dark, and there's a *lot* of dark to explore in the underbelly of this small town, but it also thrives on knowing humor and much wokeness. And for us, Dramedy + Wokeness = Excellence.

SCOOP! FACTS:

Archie Comics has been around a looooonnnnng time. Like your grandma and grandpa probably read *Archie*. It's changed over time, obvs.

When it started in the 1950s, it was apple pie on steroids. Bright, Polaroid-saturated colors, cloudless skies, and saccharine sweet. Everyone had the same face, only their Technicolor hair and clothes were different. Many of your faves were there: Archie, Betty, Veronica, and Jughead. But it never veered off the story line of the Betty-Archie-Veronica love triangle, with Jughead just wanting to eat. Their clothing style changed with time, but everything else retained that sticky sweetness. It was like they, and all of Riverdale, were frozen in time.

In the '90s, sales began to fall, because BORING. Marvel and DC were pounding them. But eventually, a new CEO arrived and BOOM! things got much cooler. They were finally willing to explore more adult themes, portraying issues like gun control, politics, financial recessions, long-term relationships, and same-sex marriage. Which is awesome because the new, improved *Life with Archie* gave us Kevin Keller! Who became a senator! We are so here for that. The series ended in 2014 when some loon tried to shoot Kevin, and Archie took the bullet to save him.

SQUISH!

Undeterred, the Archie Comic peeps came out with *Afterlife with Archie,* getting us a lot closer to our jam, *Riverdale*. It was complete zombie realness when Sabrina Spellman, the teenage witch, tried to revive Jughead's beloved floof, Hot Dog, but the spell got borked, no pun intended. The point is, when they saw everyone's response to the darker, creeptastic Archie, they knew they had a good thing.

Riverdale took the ball and ran with it. And they're serving up ALL the things, and we are shook. It's a small town, and yet there are drug runners and murderers. We take that back. We mean *murderers galore*. Don't forget cults, lots of empty coffins, organ theft, evil nuns, gryphons, gargoyle kings, and conversion therapy, which, last time we checked, was a bunch of snake oil. How all this goes down in such a wee town is beyond us, and you've got to wonder if it isn't sort of like when 1700s Paris emptied their prisons into Louisiana.

It's completely bananas, and we love it! Still,

we have *lots* of questions . . . Like, why did poor Svenson have to die when he'd already lost all his fam as a kid? Will Jughead ever publish a novel? And how does Veronica get her eyebrows so perfect?!?

We'll have to wait before we get all those answers, except for the main one: The cast of *Riverdale* tackled a story that everyone knows, and characters everyone *thinks* they know. Cole Sprouse, KJ Apa, Cami Mendes, Lili Reinhart, Ashleigh Murray, Madelaine Petsch, Casey Cott, and Charles Melton faced an enormous challenge to make it their own.

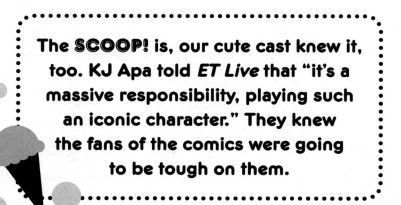

The **SCOOP!** is, our cute cast knew it, too. KJ Apa told *ET Live* that "it's a massive responsibility, playing such an iconic character." They knew the fans of the comics were going to be tough on them.

Some of those very fans are in the cast. Who, you ask? Well, Madelaine Petsch is a huge stan and got so thrilled when she was cast as Cheryl Blossom that she started crying!

Then we've got Cole Sprouse, who worked in a comic-book store! He knew all the deets about Archie Comics and had doubts about their ability to pull it off. "I come from a comic background . . . and when you hear about a dark and gritty take on an otherwise beloved franchise, that's all the wrong buzzwords for the right project," he told *The Last Magazine*.

But after he did his homework, he began to see the light. Or the dark. "It seemed like the road [in the Archie universe] had been paved for a while for something like this. My knowledge now is that the Archie universe is wide enough for something like this to take place."

Not only has *Riverdale* taken place, but everyone is shooketh! Peeps are devoted to this show, and we get it.

> We have such a super cute
> **SCOOP!** for you . . .
> Cole told *MTV News*, "We'll get
> grannies and grampies coming
> up to us and being like 'you guys
> have done a really good job.'"

Well, there you have it. KJ, Lili, Cami, Madelaine, Ashleigh, Casey, Charles, and Cole took on that responsibility and made the characters their own. The Archie Comics fans love it, and even your grandma approves.

How did they do it? Let's take a close look at each of our cutie castmates in the next chapter and see how their journey got them to the perfect part!

CHAPTER 2

CLASSMATES AND CASTMATES

*J*ust who are these gorgeous people that make up the *Riverdale* universe? How did they find themselves cast—and cast perfectly, we might add—as these iconic characters? We're going to take a deep dive into the deets on each one. Kind of like a rap sheet, which is fitting since everyone in *Riverdale* is a suspect at one point or another. We think they're all equally adorbs, and *Riverdale* is, after all, set in high school, so we'll take them on in first name alphabetical order.

Ashleigh Murray as Josie McCoy

💜 💜 💜

Born Ashleigh Monique Murray in Kansas City, Missouri, on January 18, 1988.

Astrological Sign

CAPRICORN!
Ambitious and determined, yes, but loving tradition and reserve; very polite and friendly

Ashleigh was about ten when she decided she wanted to be an actress. Lots of her costars got their calling early as well, so it's no wonder they all bonded right away! Ashleigh did school plays, then jumped into competitive drama in high school. She had a southern accent that she worked hard to change when she got to college in New York. Now *that* takes determination.

Change it she did, and she soon landed roles in films like *Welcome to New York*. But the jobs weren't coming fast enough, and funds were low.

If she ran out of money, she'd have to go back to Missouri. But that was "not an option," according to Ashleigh. She was about to get a full-time job and give up acting. Then her agent called her to audition for *Riverdale*.

She's so grateful for what she has and is the first person to say, just like Josie, that she worked very, very hard to get there! She gets it. It's part of why she understood when Josie told Archie that she didn't want the Pussycats to play his songs. But ever the friendly Capricorn, she didn't play that scene as angry. Polite, but firm. No! You've got to work hard for a long time and make sure it's your work if you want to shine.

Just like talented and ambitious Josie, Ashleigh is already reaching new heights. We know Josie is leaving *Riverdale*, which got us all squishy, but squish not! We're going to see even more Ashleigh as Josie in *Katie Keene*, another character from the Archieverse. It's a dramedy about four aspiring art-ists chasing their dreams in New York City!

Camila Mendes as Veronica Lodge

♥ ♥ ♥

Born Camila Carraro Mendes in Charlottesville, Virginia, on June 29, 1994.

Astrological Sign

CANCER!
Loves to nurture, wears their heart on their sleeve

Cami is Brazilian, and she speaks fluent Portuguese as her parents were both born and raised there. She even lived there for a year, but moved more than sixteen times in her childhood. Like Veronica, she knows what it's like to be the new kid in town!

Our girl C went the academic route and attended New York University Tisch School of the Arts—same as Cole! She knew who he was, and would see him around campus, but he doesn't remember her at all! A bit awkward? No, Cami's all good, saying, "Cole always laughs when I tell him that because I remember meeting him on certain occasions and he doesn't. I'm always like, 'Fine! Whatever! Sorry I'm not a child star!'"

Def not a child star! Cami's first role, other than an Ikea ad, was . . . you guessed it. Veronica Lodge.

One of the reasons she loves playing Ronnie? On auditions for other roles, the producers would try to push an urban typecast on her Latina heritage. With V, "she was Latina, and they weren't trying to push any stereotype on her. She just was Latina, which is how I feel."

Another thing in common with Veronica? She is 100 percent fearless. V can drop her parents and take over the Chock'lit Shoppe, and Cami is feeling her independence, too. In addition to starring with our boy Noah Centineo in *The Perfect Date*, Cami can also be seen in *The New Romantic*. Go, V! We mean C!

Casey Cott as Kevin Keller

♥ ♥ ♥

Born Casey Morton Cott in Chagrin Falls, Ohio, on August 8, 1992.

Astrological Sign

LEO!
Those lions love the spotlight, and they're fun.

Casey was in local theater productions like *Romeo and Juliet* and attended Boston University for two years before going hardcore and transferring to Carnegie Mellon University School of Drama.

Casey was cast as Kevin Keller during his last year at CM. What's so rad about Kevin is that he is the first openly gay character in the Archie Comics. KK premiered in 2010, and we are psyched that he is here. Jon Goldwater, Archie Comics co-CEO, wanted a woke world for *Riverdale*, and especially wanted to destigmatize homosexuality. "*Riverdale* has always been a safe world for everyone," he says.

Yassssss!! Our gen is waking the world and we are hyped!

It's a huge opportunity to do right by Kevin, and CC is honored to have the role. "I have a lot of joy and pride in playing Kevin," Cott told *TVGuide.com.* "I think Kevin is such a well-rounded, created character. He's smart, witty, and he's so hysterical. He's loyal."

ON CARNEGIE MELLON UNIVERSITY SCHOOL OF DRAMA

💜 **CMU School of Drama** is the *bomb*, a straight-up A+ prestige drama school.

💜 **Founded in 1914,** it's the oldest degree-granting program in the United States.

💜 **Both their graduate** and undergraduate programs are consistently ranked as being one of the top five drama programs in the country.

💜 **Alumni include** Leslie Odom Jr. (*Hamilton*), Josh Gad, Ethan Hawke, Holly Hunter (a list of all her awards would take another book!), and everybody's fave bartender, Sam Malone. Oops, we mean Ted Danson.

Charles Melton as Reggie Mantle

♥ ♥ ♥

Born Charles Michael Melton in Juneau, Alaska, on January 4, 1991.

Astrological Sign

CAPRICORN!
Ambitious, determined, and businesslike.
Def Reggie. But Charles?

CM comes from a very diverse background, considering he is of Korean, Cherokee, and European descent. He moved around a lot as a kid because his dad was in the military, and we can't help but wonder if he and Cami M. bonded over that similarity. He went to Kansas State University and even played football there, but after two years he decided to move to Los Angeles and give it a go. Well, it went!

He first got modeling gigs for Kenneth Cole, MAC, and Dolce&Gabbana. Well, duh. That face!

That face and his football days make him ideal

for playing Reggie, a jock with a love of pranks!

But like all the cast, Charles has put his own spin on things. In the comics, Reggie and Archie are frenemies, but in the new, improved *Riverdale*, Reggie goes from a rival to "the ally that Archie finds . . . when it comes to protecting Riverdale."

Charles can bring his own experiences into play in portraying that transition! Way back in 2012, CM shared some less-than-kind body-shaming tweets, and whoa, does he regret it. He made a statement saying, "I'm truly sorry for making inconsiderate comments several years ago and apologize to anyone I hurt." He said, "What I posted and said was immature, offensive, and inappropriate. I am ashamed of how I acted and there is no excuse for that behavior."

We've always felt like the coolest peeps aren't the ones who never do anything wrong (they don't exist, anyway)—the coolest can apologize for past mistakes directly, honestly, and without any of that "sorry you feel that way" tap dancing.

Well done, Charles!

Cole Sprouse as Jughead Jones

♥ ♥ ♥

Born Cole Mitchell Sprouse in Arezzo, Italy (so swass!), on August 4, 1992.

Astrological Sign

ANOTHER LEO!
Makes total sense . . . supremely talented, enthusiastic, and dramatic!

Cole has been at this for eons, right? Since he was eight months old. No wonder he's so good at his craft. We know a bit about him already from his days as Cody Martin in . . . well, in so many things!

Cole was named after legendary jazz pianist and vocalist Nat King Cole (1919–1965).

Natch you know that Cole Sprouse has an identical twin, Dylan. But did you know that the first time Cole ever appeared in a role without his brother was as Ross's son, Ben, on *Friends*?

What we think is completely cool is that the current incarnation of Jughead is similar to Cole, at least as far as being a reflective thinker. Dude had sorta lost interest in acting and had enrolled at New York University, taking archeology and photography courses. He even had a job in an artifact laboratory in Brooklyn. But Hollywood came calling, and the *Riverdale* peeps asked him to audition for the role of Archie. Instead, CS asked to do the outcast Juggy, who wasn't even supposed to be a main character. Once they vibed on Cole's moody read, they not only expanded the role, but made him less of a jokester and more like Cole!

"Suite life" indeed!

ON COLE SPROUSE'S NAMESAKE

♥ *Nat King Cole* recorded more than a hundred songs that were absolute hits on the pop charts.

♥ *He was the* first African American man to host an American television series.

♥ *In 1956 Cole* was assaulted on stage during a concert in Birmingham, Alabama, by racists and hurt his back when he fell from his piano bench.

♥ *No one has* come close to Nat King Cole's success at Capitol Records since.

♥ *Cole also acted* in television and films, and even performed on Broadway.

KJ Apa as Archie Andrews

♥ ♥ ♥

Born Keneti James Fitzgerald Apa in Auckland, New Zealand, on June 17, 1997.

Astrological Sign

GEMINI!
So, basically "bright, quick-witted, and the proverbial life of the party."

It seems Apa was destined to play music-loving Archie because he is a musician himself! And music has always been a big part of his life.

KJ's chiseled abs don't hurt, either, because whoever got this part had to live up to Kevin Keller exclaiming, "Archie got hot!!" One tough part of being Archie, though, is that KJ is SO not a redhead in real life. Which makes sense, given his Samoan ancestry, but it makes getting into character a rough two-and-a-half-hour-long, salon-chair nightmare!! He told *Vulture* that "it was really painful the first and the second time I got it done because they do my eyebrows as well . . . I had two holes—they burnt into my skin."

We guess this is the definition of suffering for your art! Speaking of pain . . .

Here's a small **SCOOP!** for you . . .
KJ actually broke his hand shooting
the scene where he punches through
the ice to save Cheryl Blossom. And hid
it from his fellow castmates!
He was so in the moment he just
kept going. MOOD!

Lili Reinhart as Betty Cooper

♥ ♥ ♥

Born Lili Pauline Reinhart in Cleveland, Ohio, on September 13, 1996.

Astrological Sign

VIRGO!

Modest and humane with great attention to detail, mostly to help those around them. Could this BE any more Betty Cooper??

Lili also was very young when she got the acting bug and began studying and auditioning by the age of ten. But nothing good comes too easily, and our Betty Cooper is living proof! She moved to Los Angeles at eighteen to pursue her dreams—and like all dreams, things got wonky. LA is a tough town, and Lili almost bolted after five months! She has been super candid about her struggles with her mental health and even told *W Magazine* that she went back to Cleveland to see a therapist who helped her find calm again.

Here's where Lily's story gets really wacky. It was at this time that Lili auditioned for *Riverdale*. Since she was back in her home hood she sent in a tape, and given that she had some further personal healing to do, it didn't take. She was passed over. But then, *kaboom!*

"Somehow, I revved myself up," she said. "I was like, 'I've wanted this for so long. I went out there, failed, and now I'm going to try it again.' I didn't work my ass off for one try."

Girl went back to Tinseltown and nailed the in-person audition.

Of course she did.

We wonder if the talented Lili's own experiences are part of why she's so good at playing not just the sweet, bubbly Betty C., but also the darker, complicated Ms. Cooper. We are SO here for it!

Madelaine Petsch as Cheryl Blossom

♥ ♥ ♥

Born Madelaine Grobbelaar Petsch in Port Orchard, Washington, on August 18, 1994.

Astrological Sign

LEO (ANOTHER LION?!!)
Of course! Fiery, unafraid, and FUN.

Madelaine, much like her alter ego Cheryl, knows what she wants. Ballet at three, theater classes at five—MP began sprinting right out of the gate. She graduated from Tacoma School of the Arts and then BAM! was off to LA. She worked THREE jobs to make ends meet—coffee shop manager, photography assistant, and hookah lounge waitress—and got some small roles in films like *The Hive*, and even a Coca-Cola ad campaign.

Eventually, she auditioned for *Riverdale* . . . to play Betty!! The casting directors knew their jam, though, and said, "Idts! You are SO Cheryl."

How Cheryl is MP?

28

HERE'S THE SCOOP!

Madelaine's hair is naturally that fab red, just like CB's. But here's the kicker: She was bullied as a kid for that hair. So not only was she able to relate to Cheryl's insecurities and sense of isolation that made her so, well . . . snipey, to put it nicely, but playing CB also gave her closure on the experience of being bullied.

"After playing Cheryl, I realized the bullying doesn't come from anything but insecurities in oneself. The people who are bullying you, they're insecure about who they are and that's why they're bullying you. It never has to do with the person they're bullying," Madelaine told *Stylecaster* in 2017.

BONUS! Obvs, MP was born to play CB!

SCOOP! QUIZ

WHOSE LINE IS IT?

We've SCOOPed ways in which our cute cast-mates resemble and have even influenced their *Riverdale* roles! Can you tell whether the following lines were said by the *Riverdale* character or the actor who portrays the character?

1 "If I dyed my hair, my mother would actually disown me."

MADELAINE PETSCH   **OR**   CHERYL BLOSSOM?

2 "The best stuff happens when you take a chance."

LILI REINHART   **OR**   BETTY COOPER?

3 "I was sad and in a dark place, and I turned to a hobby to sort of take me out of that."

COLE SPROUSE   OR   JUGHEAD JONES?

4 "Sardonic humor is just my way of relating to the world."

COLE SPROUSE   OR   JUGHEAD JONES?

5 "You can't go through life trying not to get hurt."

KJ APA   OR   ARCHIE ANDREWS?

6 "Can't we, in this post–James Franco world, be all things at once?"

CAMILA MENDES OR VERONICA LODGE?

7 "Everybody wants a seat at the table, but nobody wants to give up space."

ASHLEIGH MURRAY OR JOSIE MCCOY?

8 "What was it like before she got here? I honestly cannot remember."

CASEY COTT OR KEVIN KELLER?

9 "I do everything for everyone."

LILI REINHART **OR** BETTY COOPER?

10 "In case you haven't noticed, I'm weird."

COLE SPROUSE **OR** JUGHEAD JONES?

11 "Take care of yourself in every way that you can."

CAMILA MENDES **OR** VERONICA LODGE?

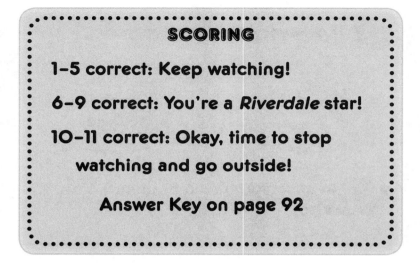

SCORING

1-5 correct: Keep watching!

6-9 correct: You're a *Riverdale* star!

10-11 correct: Okay, time to stop watching and go outside!

Answer Key on page 92

CHAPTER 3

NOT JUST PRETTY FACES

*N*ow that we know all our players, and the ingenious ways they brought a bit of themselves to their parts (as well as sometimes outright resemble the characters!), it's time to rip off those masks! You know they aren't the characters they play, so let's do a deep SCOOP! into traits—some fun and quirky, some serious and thoughtful— that they don't get to show while playing their alter egos. In some ways, they're the polar opposite of their characters. And thank goodness for that! There is WAY too much murder and mayhem in *Riverdale* for real life. And we want our cutie cast to stay out of lockup!!

We'll start with the obvious: Cami doesn't come from a Social Register society family in New York.

Luckily she doesn't have to try to put her dad in jail, either! Talk about conflict of interest!

Looks-wise CM has a stunning face that resembles V's, but Cami doesn't have jet-black hair and isn't always polished and super styled like Veronica. She likes "clothes that I can move in and feel good in." Her locks are a divine natural brown.

She is, however, a sensitive sweetheart like V. That sensitivity is a wonderful attribute because it makes one a great friend—empathic and kind. At the same time, it can mean your heart is on your sleeve, and lead to insecurity. At one point Cami was so hard on herself she developed an eating disorder. But here's how this rad girl handles it: by helping others. Yes, please!

She talks about her eating disorder openly, posting online about body positivity, hoping to make her fans who have similar issues feel less alone and more likely to get help. And you know how good begets good? Well CM has the MOOD down. Helping her fans has helped her!

"I've been kinder to myself because of all the positive feedback. I think all the encouragement from fans, and how much I see that they're going through the same thing, and how much I feel like I actually have an opportunity here to inspire people and prevent people from going down that path, has shown me I actually could make that difference in someone's life," Camila told *Seventeen* in 2018.

We absolutely ADORE Cami! And it's not just us who feel that way . . . Lili Reinhart and Cami are tight! We'll go over that more in later chapters, but there's something important they have in common: They speak openly about their issues, hoping to help others. Lili has def been forthcoming about her anxiety and speaks highly of therapy—because it helps! She also had some things to say about body positivity, because yes, even TV stars have fluctuating weight. Speaking at the *Glamour* Women of the Year Summit she said, "Remind yourself that this perfect world you see online, in magazines, in movies and TV, is presented to you through many different filters. So do not set impossible goals of meeting those fake standards."

Preach, Lili!

We think Betty would be out there advocating, too, if there was not so much cray cray happening in *Riverdale*. Cray case in point—her mom! Mrs. Cooper is a bit . . . off. So she and Betty aren't super close, which is the opposite of Ms. Reinhart. LR is a self-proclaimed mama's girl!

"My mom is like my best friend. I tell her everything and we're extremely close," Lili says.

Lili is also close friends with Madelaine Petsch, so close that they were even roomies during the first season! Clearly a bit different than Betty and Cheryl's frenemy-ship. There are other diffs, too. In the original comics, Cheryl was only around for two years, because she was deemed too shmexy. And while our *Riverdale* Cheryl is def sticking around, she's still pretty spicy, and sometimes not so nice. But Miss Madelaine couldn't be nerdier or sweeter! She likes guys who read, and says, "I've kind of been typecast—I'm not as mean as people think I would be. I'm the complete opposite and I want people to know they can always approach me." In fact, she started her whole YouTube channel just to show that she's a nice person!

Speaking of nice, Cole Sprouse had words for his friends that seem impossible to imagine coming from Jughead: "Casey, you are a master of conversation. Your desired outcome is never something selfish, it's always wholesome and pure, and you are a master of making people feel better through talking." Awwww, happy squish!

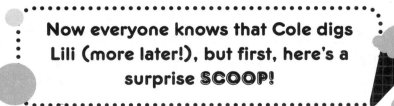

Now everyone knows that Cole digs Lili (more later!), but first, here's a surprise SCOOP!

When he first accepted the role of JJ, he "argued creatively" that the character should be asexual, kind of like the comic book character whose true love is food! He knows *Riverdale* would do justice to the orientation and treat it with sensitivity.

They also treat Kevin Keller's orientation with tact and respect, and even though Casey isn't gay, he took care to make sure that KK wasn't just the GBF stereotype. Everyone loves Kevin, and Casey made sure that Kevin was fully realized; his sexuality is an important part of his character but doesn't define him. "That's what makes playing Kevin such a joy," he says.

We know Casey has fun playing Kevin because it's so fun to watch him! And do you know who's jelly? KJ Apa! Even though he gets to be the heartthrob all the girls pine for, he said he'd love for Archie to have a gay story line. KJ spoke out for LGBT rights when an Aussie rugby player made rude, homophobic comments on one of KJ's Instagram posts. We are proud of him for using his platform so well!

Since KJ kicks it as Archie, we figured he must've had a similar high school experience, but nope—

it was a steep learning curve. Coming from New Zealand, American culture was totally foreign to him, and he says, "I tell people our schools in New Zealand are most similar to Hogwarts." Whoa. So does an owl bring you the acceptance letter?

SCOOP! FACTS:
KJ is also half Samoan, and his dad is a matai—which is a chief! No wonder he got the role of Archie, the veritable chief of the *Riverdale* universe.

Both KJ and Archie are musicians, but KJ says his taste is more in line with Van Halen and Third Eye Blind than the softer stuff Archie likes. And soon we'll get to know more about the music Ashleigh Murray likes herself, as opposed to only hearing Josie and the Pussycats songs. When she and KJ took the stage at FVDED in the Park in British Columbia, it was a life-changer. She tweeted, "So I just sang onstage, in front of 20,000+ people, for the first time ever. With the good graces of @kj_apa and Kygo. I'm still shaking.

I've decided, I'm going to start taking lessons and making my own music." We can't wait to hear her first album and love how *Riverdale* is inspiring its stars to aspire to even bigger things!

Another thing to love about *Riverdale* (there are lots!) is how woke it is. Sadly, not everyone is, and we were so upset to hear that Internet trolls attacked Ashleigh Murray online about Josie's story line with Archie, and a lot of it was racially motivated. SO. NOT. OK. We're not sure how long it will take more people to wake up, but we hope it's soon. Can we hurry up, please?

Speaking of moral evolution, we already noted that Charles Melton experienced some of his own, publicly apologizing for body-shaming tweets. It seems Reggie is experiencing some, too, and rather than being the boorish dolt he was in Season 1, he's become a reliable, kind help to Veronica. Even though it hasn't worked out for R & V (so far), CM told *Entertainment Weekly*, "Hopefully we can turn some Varchie fans into

Veggie fans after they see the kiss and really see how much Reggie cares about Veronica." Hmmmm . . . wethinks perhaps Charles is wisely putting some of his own feelings into his portrayal of Reggie Mantle. More on that next, as we check out the cast's love lives!

ON SAMOA . . .

Samoa, a gorgeous Polynesian island in the South Pacific, has only one city. And it's named Apia! Hmmmmm . . .

Nine volcanic islands make up Samoa, and two of them, Savai'i and Upolu, comprise more than 99 percent of the country. The entire country is within the "ring of fire," an area in the Pacific where tons of volcanic eruptions and earthquakes occur! EEK!

Men are the ones who cook and prepare for holidays in Samoan culture. Does this mean KJ can grill a burger as mean as Pop's??

CHAPTER 4

LOVE IN THE TIME OF *RIVERDALE*

*I*t's a many-splendored thing, but for the *Riverdale* cuties, love is confusing. Because how can you find compatibility with a partner when their parents are murderers, mobsters, or cult members? Hard to keep love alive in this hard-knock town. Hard to keep *anyone* alive in this hard-knock town. Wait, which town do we mean, Hollywood or Riverdale?? Well, both, which is apt here because the *Riverdale* gang has found love on both sides of the camera.

Shall we start with the obvs? Or perhaps not too obvs, because we can't exactly tell what's going on here. Everyone is shipping Bughead, and rightly so. They have each other's back, total loyalty. They work well together, and we know common interests are a huge glue for couples, even if those interests are a murder board! And that *Romeo and Juliet* ladder-to-her window scene? We're awwwwwwing!

Surely you know about Bughead's IRL romance, Sprousehart? While they don't want to hide the fact that they're dating, they do want to keep the actual deets of the relationship private. They talk heaps about the art they make together, though. He's an accomplished photographer; she's often his muse. So like Bughead, they have that working interest in common, and that's open for discussion.

Cole posted a gorge photo of Lili lying in the snow of all places, with the caption: "'How do the people you shoot even tolerate you?' —@lilireinhart on making her suffer for my art." They're having a great time making said art, and want the world to know. So why don't they want us to know about their 'ship? "I think it's just that I'm so protective over it," Lili says. "It's not something the world needs to know about, because if you give them anything, they are just going to want more."

Spot on. We do want to know more! But it looks like it's an ongoing process, with rumored breakups, and then Sprousehart both clapping back when said breakup is reported. So what's happening now? We have no idea! And we're okay with that! Shipping celebs is all well and good, but when we decide they owe us time and deets on their lives is when it gets problematic for everyone.

While things are shaky in Riverdale for Veggie, it does seem that Camila and Charles are a real thing, too. There must be some kind of kismet with people named Camila (or Camilla) and Charles!

And just in case you didn't know, we're talking HRHs here . . .

His and Her Royal Highness of England.

47

HERE'S THE SCOOP!

ON THE OG CHARLES AND CAMILLA

- ♥ *Prince Charles was* the first royal heir to earn a university degree.

- ♥ *Charles and Camilla,* then Camilla Shand, were introduced at a mutual friend's event in 1971 and began dating.

- ♥ *He left to* join the Royal Navy, and when he came back—she was engaged to another guy!

- ♥ *He founded* The Prince of Wales's Charitable Fund in 1979, which awards grants to assist causes such as the environment, education, and sustainability.

- ♥ *He was one* of the first people to champion the environment, and has been doing so for forty years.

- ♥ **He was initially** derided for supporting these causes.

- ♥ **Everyone misses** Princess Diana, and Charles was devastated by her death despite the fact that they were divorced.

- ♥ **Charles flew to** Paris upon the news of Diana's death to bring her body back to London.

- ♥ **He has written** books on the natural world and the environment including *Harmony* and *Climate Change*.

- ♥ **Several of his** vehicles have been converted to RUN ON WINE!

- ♥ **Charles and Camilla** married in a civil ceremony in Windsor in April 2005, thirty-four years after first meeting.

- ♥ **Charles and Camilla** live at Highgrove House, which also has a home farm that grows organic food, and even launched the organic food company Duchy Originals.

Now leaving London and back to Riverdale . . . Charmila are a LOT more open about their relationship than Sprousehart. Right out of the gate they posted adorbs pics of a trip to South Korea, like the two of them wearing bunny hats on stunning Myeongdong Street. We want to go to there! They just celebrated their one-year anniversary in August 2019, and have even hit the Met Gala together. It makes sense that C & C go together so well. She's a Cancer and he's a Capricorn. Astrology.com says when these two signs meet "this relationship builds and grows from a strong foundation of material and emotional security." Awww, squish!

Cami says she is an open person and doesn't like hiding. "But the more I get used to this lifestyle the more I reevaluate what I want to share and what I don't." We respect that, so we'll move on from Charmila. *But first . . .*

> **Here's a super cute SCOOP! for you: Charles told *Cosmopolitan* that he was thinking about Cami when he auditioned for the role of deeply-in-love Daniel in *The Sun Is Also a Star*. Swoonworthy!**

Now we're wondering who the rest of the cast cuties might be thinking about during steamy love scenes on *Riverdale* . . . or even auditions for love scenes somewhere less noir!

Say, for example, when Ashleigh Murray auditions, does she access feelings for a special someone to make it ring true? We don't know if Ashleigh prefers method acting, but we *do* know that there is a handsome mystery man all over her Insta. Who is he?? All we know is she captioned one of their pics together: "Low key never thought I'd find a human that makes me glow like Claire Danes in *Stardust*. He totally, totally does." There are also recent pics of them attending a wedding together in Ireland. She clearly wants to keep her private life private, and we are totally down with it. And we are totally happy for her!

Madelaine Petsch, however, is totes open about her relationship with singer Travis Mills, so much so that he even appears on her YouTube channel, helping her pick out her outfit for Beautycon! She told *Access Hollywood*, "I just keep my relationship really public, so I don't think people really care, which is kind of weird and a catch-22. I feel like if I just keep myself open, and I'm not telling them everything about my relationship, but people know I'm in one, I don't hide it, then people don't really care."

Ummmm, yes we do! We are psyched for you, too, but plan to give you private space as well! This is the best catch-22 we can think of!

So what about our last two singletons, Casey and KJ? They both have had a pretty private dating history and seem philosophical about it all. "The thing is, I don't think it matters whether you're looking for a relationship or not—it's not for us to decide when we meet the love of our lives," KJ told *Seventeen*.

Well, then I guess they're still on the market. Or are they????

KJ was recently spotted at Comic-Con being super cuddly with Britt Robertson. If the name sounds familiar, it's because he costarred with her in 2017's *A Dog's Purpose*. You could almost say they're childhood sweethearts. Or not, but it's still sweet. They've also been seen hanging out with his *Riverdale* mates. If he's bringing her around the crew, we think it might be serious!

Time will tell. And since Casey likes to keep his love life on the down-low, he'll be the first to get our picks on WHAT, WHERE, WHY & WHO would be the perfect dates for the cast.

DATING GAME

Since we've SCOOPed so much about "Love in the Time of *Riverdale*," we're going all out with our best guesses on...

what · where · why · & who

would be a great date for our *Riverdale* cast-mates . . .

Casey Cott

WHO—Halle Bailey

WHAT—A night at the theater

WHERE—The Majestic Theater, NYC

WHY—They both have a musical theater background! Also, Casey is a Leo, Halle an Aries—despite their sometimes noisy differences, Aries often looks to Leo as a guide or counselor.

KJ Apa

WHO—Joss Stone

WHAT—Concerts!

WHERE—Glastonbury Festival, UK!

WHY—Both his character Archie and his character Griffin from *The Last Summer* are great musicians. We figure since he has so much in common with Archie and Griffin, maybe the strong and soulful Joss would be his perfect musical match!

Ashleigh Murray

WHO—That mystery man all over her Instagram

WHAT—Their wedding

WHERE—Ireland, where a friend of theirs wed. And she has said she's "completely in love with Ireland."

WHY—We SCOOPed her Insta post about him, and if anyone says they've found "a human that makes me glow like Claire Danes in *Stardust*," they need to stay together!

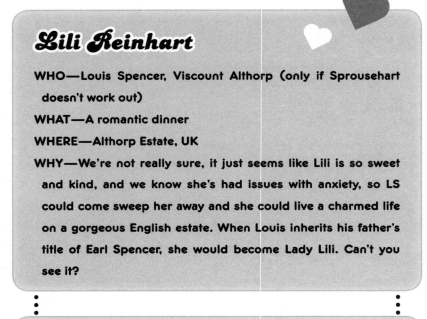

Lili Reinhart

WHO—Louis Spencer, Viscount Althorp (only if Sprousehart doesn't work out)

WHAT—A romantic dinner

WHERE—Althorp Estate, UK

WHY—We're not really sure, it just seems like Lili is so sweet and kind, and we know she's had issues with anxiety, so LS could come sweep her away and she could live a charmed life on a gorgeous English estate. When Louis inherits his father's title of Earl Spencer, she would become Lady Lili. Can't you see it?

Camila Mendes

WHO—Noah Centineo (only if Charmila doesn't work out)

WHAT—Charity dinner

WHERE—Rainforest Cafe

WHY—We SCOOPed him, too—and he's such a nice guy! They both donated toward relief from the Amazon fires and looked adorbs together in *The Perfect Date*, and NC is nothing like Brooks Rattigan, the player.

Charles Melton

WHO—Yara Shahidi (again, only if no Charmila)

WHAT—Fun and flirty dinner

WHERE—Grand Central Oyster Bar in Grand Central Station, New York City

WHY—Yet again blurring the line between fiction and reality, we just thought they looked so cute together in *The Sun Is Also a Star*.

Cole Sprouse

WHO—Lorde (you know what we're going to say in these parentheses)

WHAT—Art gallery date

WHERE—A Garry Winogrand exhibition so they can groove on his spectacular technical skill and brilliant eye for catching the '60s in photographs.

WHY—Introspective, artsy, and intelligent like Cole . . . but who are we kidding? We'll never recover if he and Lili break up. #Bugspart Forever! Yes, we made that up, too!

CHAPTER 5

SQUAD GOALS

*W*e've surmised that the casting directors of *Riverdale* must be some of the most talented in their field. Not just because they chose people who feel like the perfect match to both their comic counterparts and series characters, but also because they chose actors who they must've felt would have incredible chemistry together.

We're here to SCOOP! that it's not just on the screen. These people are #squadgoals IRL!!

We've already mentioned that Madelaine and Lili are so close they were roommates during the first season.

But here's a secret SCOOP! for you . . . and this SCOOP! falls under the "don't try this at home" PSA.

MP and LR were so close that Lili would pop MP's blackheads for her! We're kind of grossed out and charmed at the same time! Madelaine says that "Lili was actually the person who got me on a good skincare game and taught me about the steps you're supposed to take." That is true friendship right there.

MP comes to her friends' defense when needed, too, saying that she was "blown away" and impressed when Lili and Cole clapped back on the tabloids vulturing their (maybe) breakup with some savage Insta captions alongside their recent *W Magazine* cover story pic. She also says, "We all got on the group text like, 'Oh my god! That was so cool!'"

Of course they have a group thread!

Lili has talked about how the meteoric rise of *Riverdale*'s popularity has forged super close bonds. "I think that's a bond that [the *Riverdale* cast] has created as well, and you just don't let go of. I've made friends in this show that I will have hopefully until the day I die," she told *Who What Wear*. More happy squishes!

We're pretty sure bonds like this don't easily break, and whether or not Sprousehart remain a couple, the friendship will stay strong. Especially when they say things like this about each other:

"Cole is the smartest person that I'm friends with," Lili shares. "He's incredibly passionate—about art, about photography, about acting— and I really admire that."

"[Lili's] one of those people that consistently pushes me to be better at the arts that I'm pursuing, and that's just the kind of person she is. She inspires excellence out of everybody she works with."

We already SCOOPed what Cole has to say about Casey, and Casey returns the love:

"He is . . . underneath his dark, moody, artsy self, quite a fun, youthful guy that just loves making people happy."

And about Lili? Casey waxes poetic!

"Extremely sweet, and passionate, and kind, and goofy, and authentic."

Lili and Cami are mega-close as well.

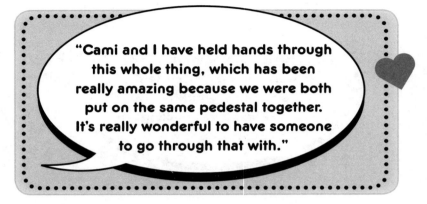

"Cami and I have held hands through this whole thing, which has been really amazing because we were both put on the same pedestal together. It's really wonderful to have someone to go through that with."

Friends who give together, stick together—and the *Riverdale* castmates are on the case!

Cami and Madelaine both donated to relief efforts for the Amazon rainforest fires through Rainforest Alliance, and Cami nominated none other than Charles Melton to donate as well! And we already filled you in about Lili and Cami speaking openly about eating disorders and body positivity.

But we have more wholesome details to share about this charitable bunch!

Cami works with Project HEAL to raise funds for others recovering from eating disorders, and Lili partnered with Aerie for contributions to the National Eating Disorders Association.

They both also had something to say about the fact that *Cosmopolitan Philippines* Photoshopped their pictures too heavily. "Camila and I have worked incredibly hard to feel confident and comfortable in the bodies that we have. It's an everyday battle sometimes. And to see our bodies become so distorted in an editing process is a perfect example of the obstacles we have yet to overcome."

We couldn't be prouder of the cast for giving back, and we urge everyone to listen to their words on these issues. Don't believe those airbrushed and distorted photos you see, and certainly don't compare yourself to them! We're all perfectly imperfect. And most important: Be kind to yourself!

We're serious.

But the cast isn't always serious. Which makes sense. After the intense mood on *Riverdale*, they need to let their hair down. Or at least back to its natural color (we couldn't resist that—*Riverdale* loves its bright tones)!

They clearly have a blast together. In group interviews, they are constantly—and hilariously—ribbing one another.

Teen Vogue shot a video of the cast playing Truth or Dare, and we thank our lucky stars they did! Because it is gold. Casey chooses dare, and Lili reads him the card to "yell out the first thing that comes to your mind." "Green!" Say huh?? But they're LOLing.

Madelaine also chooses dare, and Ashleigh reads, "Impersonate the person immediately to your left." That'd be Lili. At which point MP just morphs into a five-year-old imitating everything Lili says at that moment.

Then KJ gets the dare to do an impression of someone in the group until someone can figure out who it is. So he grabs his phone and holds it up to his face, posing and primping, and everyone yells, "Madelaine!" She happily screams, "It's me!"

Lili is then dared to pick anyone and dance with them. Without missing a beat, she gets KJ in the exact slow dance embrace from the pilot and imitates herself as Betty, saying, "So now that I'm a River Vixen, and you're on the football team, I was thinking, maybe we could, you know, be a power couple." It's done with such a wink the rest the cast is dying.

Next up is Ashleigh, who is dared to sing everything she says for the next couple of rounds. She does and, of course, sounds pitch-perfect! But then she picks a truth, which is to tell about her first kiss. She relays how she went into turtle mode, but then got brave and kissed him much longer. Then she says, "Sorry, Mom!"

So much cute! As cute as Lili being dared to speak like an alien? Equally so, we'd say, as Lili then goes on to say some gibberish that sounds a lot like when a cartoon dog shakes his head and makes that *wablahwablahwablah* sound. Did we just make that up? Yaaaas!

But wait! There are more LOLs . . . In an

interview with *ET* for Comic-Con 2019, standing behind the seated trio LR, CM, and MP, are Cole and KJ—laughing like boys in the back of class! They're poking each other, giggling, pulling looks; KJ plays with Cole's hair, and Cole even playfully head boops KJ!! It's so beyond! We half-expected them to break out into a wrestling match and would've been all for it.

The whole cast is ALL OVER one another's social media. And you've gotta check it out for yourself.

There's pool parties, karaoke, riding scooters, naps, workouts, birthday parties, commutes to Vancouver, pizza parties . . . It's all too much fun!

On Lili's Insta there's a riotous video of her, KJ, Cole, and Cami on a trampoline, where the boys are doing that thing to launch the girls sky-high, who duly take huge diggers. LR captions, "Cami falling over in slow motion is my new favorite thing." Not to be outdone, CM comes right back, commenting, "Yes but have you zoomed in on your face when you shoot up in the air 😊."

Lili also has an excellent short clip up of her in the driver's seat while the song "Red, Red, Wine" is blasting on the speakers. Then, the camera zooms in on Cole sitting in the back, absentmindedly playing with his hair. She zooms in further. He notices, looks up. Stares. Shakes his head no. We are dead.

On Madelaine's Insta we see a shot of Cole and KJ mugging away all faux shmexy, and she captions, "This is what happens when I leave my phone on set 😊."

Even KJ Apa posted a silly selfie of himself kissing Charles's face on the poster for *The Sun Is Also a Star,* captioning, "When ya bestie's face is all over the town, love ya @melton." Charles jokes back, "Get off me."

And get this—Ashleigh Murray calls Cami her "nugget." On CM's birthday, she shared a shot of the two of them, writing, "Hbd to my favorite nugget, my cherub, my camimi."

We can't awwwww enough! These people really mean it—they're like family! The easiest way to tell? Madelaine Petsch's reaction to when Cheryl Blossom is mean to someone: "It's always a dream to play the villain, but it's also so hard because [the cast] are also my best friends, right? I have to be mean to them on-screen, and afterward, I'm always hugging them. 'I didn't mean it!'"

Squad goals indeed!

SCOOP! QUIZ

WHO'S MOST LIKELY TO . . . ?

At the 2017 E! Red Carpet Awards, the cast of *Riverdale* played a game of "Most Likely to . . ."
So, how well do you know the cast of *Riverdale*?

↓ TAKE THIS SCOOP! QUIZ ↓
TO FIND OUT!

 1 Get a song stuck in their head?

_____

 2 Be found at craft services (on-set version of a deli)?

_____

3 Try to improvise their lines?

_____

4 Be late to set?

_____

5 Be super early to set?

_____

6 Bait fans on social media?

_____

7 Provide snacks?

_____

8 Work out with KJ?

_____

9 Sneak out at night?

_____

Give away a spoiler?

_____

Break character in a scene?

_____

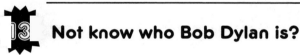

Take home an outfit?

_____

Not know who Bob Dylan is?

_____

Go "full dark no stars"?

_____

Fake their own death?

_____

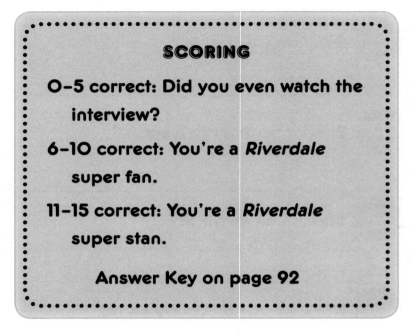

SCORING

0-5 correct: Did you even watch the interview?

6-10 correct: You're a *Riverdale* super fan.

11-15 correct: You're a *Riverdale* super stan.

Answer Key on page 92

And here are a few of SCOOP!'s very own original prompts. Write your own answers here and share with your friends (or don't)!

WHO'S MOST LIKELY TO . . .

1 Post a selfie during an earthquake?

_____

2 Bring home a stray animal?

_____

3 Throw a fit during a game of Clue?

_____

4 Bring reusable straws to everyone on set?

_____

 Complain about an ex?

 March for climate change?

 Lose their keys?

 Write a book?

 Take flying lessons?

 **Serenade someone?**

_____

 **Drop everything and travel the world?**

_____

 Get on an Elon Musk rocket and go to Mars?

_____

 **Get harassed by a ghost?**

_____

 **Get beaten up by a kangaroo?**

_____

15 Go into politics?

_____

16 Cry at a commercial with puppies in it?

_____

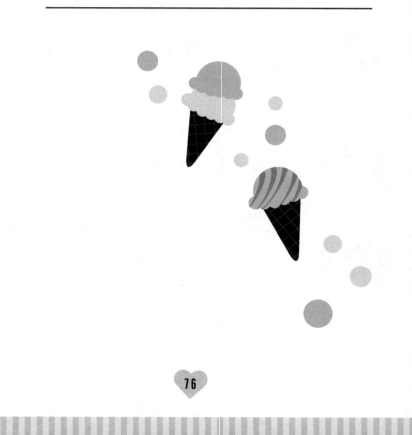

CHAPTER 6

THE TAKEAWAY

*I*n our takeaway, we always like to explore how lives have changed and get excited about what's next for the castmates. But here, we have to stop and take a moment to honor someone. By all accounts, he was a great guy and has been acting since he played a high school heartthrob, Dylan McKay, on *Beverly Hills, 90210* in the early '90s.

Luke Perry, aka Fred Andrews, suffered a massive stroke and passed away at the age of fifty-two. The *Riverdale* cast has been devastated, with Madelaine posting a heartfelt tribute to him on her Instagram: "Luke, I am so lucky to have known you & gotten so close to you these last 3 years. You were such a light in our lives; the most genuine & kind soul

I will ever know. From day one of this show you were the most amazing mentor to me. Thank you for teaching me not only about this industry, but also about kindness and being a family and how to foster and nurture those important relationships . . . you were the absolute best at that. I love you Luke, you and those sweet forehead kisses will forever be missed."

The first episode of Season 4 is titled "In Honorarium," and Roberto Aguirre-Sacasa, *Riverdale* creator and showrunner, says, "We had the table read for it and I'm not going to lie, we were all crying. It was just devastating. A father figure and mentor to the show's young cast, Luke was incredibly generous, and he infused the set with love and kindness."

KJ Apa has spoken about how Luke helped him and the cast navigate the sudden fame, as well as the pitfalls that come with it. And there are plenty of pits.

We know that's hard to imagine because it seems

everyone wants to be famous these days and strives to be at least famesque, if not famous for actually doing something. There's money, and doors swing right open for just about any heart's desire—at least materialistically. It's the inner life that takes a hit.

What can happen when you're famous is that it's hard to trust new people because you never know if they like the real you, or if they just want to hang out because you may have access to something they want.

Luckily, the cast has one another, and KJ certainly has a gang of old friends who aren't going to treat him any differently. When asked by a reporter if he's now the "cool guy" with his friends, he had a definitive answer. "Nah." Here's to keeping it 100 percent real, KJ!

Another pitfall is the lack of privacy. It's great to have people interested in you, but sometimes they lack boundaries and that admiration turns into people you don't even know expecting something from you. And getting angry when you don't live up to sometimes bizarre ideals.

Someone who has been dealing with this for decades is Cole, who explains it very intelligently. In response to people around NYU concocting unfounded rumors (stupid ones like he fell down the stairs in the library) about him to pretend they knew him, he said, "When you're a public figure, people use you to build their identities. And I think that was a bit daunting."

Sometimes people even walk up to them in public and feel entitled to ask them personal questions, or even touch them! So bonkers. No wonder many celebrities hire bodyguards. Celebrities are humans who don't owe their life to people, and fans who blur the line between fiction and reality aren't being very considerate. For someone with anxiety, like Lili, it's extra tough. "I don't know how anyone can get used to that," she's said.

We're going to guess one doesn't. We're huge fans of the cast, but always like to advise fellow fans that support>stalking.

Ashleigh Murray has some very wise words to share—essentially that overnight success is truly difficult to deal with. Given that she achieved it in her late twenties instead of early twenties, she feels for her younger costars. "I know that I would've crumbled."

We're so glad she didn't! And we'll bet her younger costars appreciate having had AM around for the last three seasons. They seem to navigate their success well!

Just in time, too. We already SCOOPed Josie is leaving *Riverdale* for the Big Apple in *Katie Keene*. Katie Keene is also a longtime Archieverse character and was originally a fashion model. In the new TV series, Katie is now an aspiring fashion designer. It won't have the same dark feel as *Riverdale*, which is good, because moving to NYC in your twenties to be any kind of creative is scary enough! Everyone is surely going to miss Josie and Ashleigh, but fret not! Not only will Josie return for the first episode of Season 4, but she'll also be in great company on *Katie Keene*, with Lucy Hale, Julia Chan, and Camille Hyde.

Seems like everyone is exploring new roles, and we are psyched for the castmates!

Charles Melton just had a star turn in *The Sun Is Also a Star,* pun completely intended, about a hopeless romantic who falls in love in one day. Sign us up!

KJ has not one but two upcoming films: *I Still Believe*, about the Christian rock star Jeremy Camp, and the thriller *Altar Rock*, about the Boston Marathon bombing. We will def be in the theaters to check them out.

Casey Cott will play a former quarterback turned mascot in *The Mascot*, and he also has *All the Little Things We Kill* coming out soon. It tells the story of a college professor who's so determined to get semiautomatic weapons banned that she takes her students hostage to force the bill. Yes, please!

The serious projects are in vogue, as our very own Cheryl, aka Madelaine Petsch, will play the victim of an assault so vicious, she is left blind, trapped in her apartment, and terrified of another assault in the upcoming thriller *Sightless*. MP will also play Clare in *Clare at 16*, about a psychopath serial killer. The fun never ends!

Cami just played the perfect dream girl in *The Perfect Date*, opposite Noah Centineo. Next up is *Coyote Lake*, where she plays a young woman who runs a bed-and-breakfast with her mother, but they have some dark secrets. Hmmmmm, sounds just a bit familiar!

Lili is making waves as one of a group of former exotic dancers who band together to take advantage of clients who have been taking advantage of them for years in *Hustlers*—to *rave* reviews. GO, BETTY! Oops . . . we mean GO, LILI!! Speaking of familiar, she's also at the top of her creative game as an executive producer of *Chemical Hearts*, playing the lead role of Grace Town, a transfer student teen who finds a new lease on life by working on her school's newspaper. We're sure there's going to be a smart new take here!

The phrase "smart new take" reminds us of Cole. This is a guy who grew up in the industry but stepped away to get a stellar education at NYU and is an accomplished photographer. He's shown himself to be a bit of an intellectual, and we are duly dazzled. Even his Instagram is a tongue-in-cheek work of art. He has an account called @camera_duels, where he secretly photographs people who think they are secretly photographing him. Recently he played a teen with cystic fibrosis in *Five Feet Apart*, and has reportedly joined the cast of the film *Silk Road*, a true-crime thriller about the Darknet. Even so, given his curiosity and cerebral interests, we can't help but wonder if Cole will be pursuing other arts in addition to acting!

But one thing we do know is he's still pursuing being Jughead Jones, thank goodness for that.

The end of Season 3 had a frightening flash forward for Juggy, but we feel sure Jones will stick around, keeping *Riverdale* an interesting, funny, and—especially—heavily narrated place, recording its trials and tribulations for all posterity. Hopefully with Betty by his side. We're kind of optimistic for Sprousehart, too.

Actually, we really have NO earthly idea what's going to happen, but that's half the fun and that's why we love *Riverdale* . . . because we really have no idea what's going on, and we wouldn't have it any other way!

WRITE YOUR OWN SCOOP!

The year is 2030, and it's the ten-year reunion for the cast . . .

1 Where is it held?

_____

_____

2 Who is hosting?

_____

_____

3 Which IRL couple is still together and married?

_____

Cole Sprouse is known for his hilarious tweets on Twitter. What are your three favorites and why?

1 _____

_____

_____

2 _____

_____

_____

3 _____

_____

_____

Rumor has it Season 5 is in the works. Write down three predictions for what will happen in the next season of *Riverdale*.

Charles Melton is starring in *Bad Boys for Life*, alongside megastar actor Will Smith. Who are some other stars you'd like to see Melton share the screen with in the future?

_____

_____

_____

_____

_____

_____

_____

_____

_____

You run into Madelaine Petsch and Camila Mendes in a coffee shop, and they invite you to sit down. What are three questions you ask them?

_____

_____

_____

_____

_____

_____

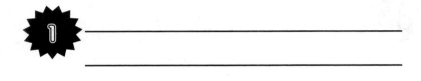

_____

_____

_____

Lili Reinhart is passionate about promoting awareness of mental health, and encouraging others to seek help when they need it. What are three causes you are passionate about?

1. _____
_____
_____

2. _____
_____
_____

3. _____
_____
_____

ANSWER KEY

♥ ♥ ♥

QUIZ #1: WHOSE LINE IS IT?

1. Madelaine Petsch
2. Lili Reinhart
3. Cole Sprouse
4. Jughead Jones
5. Archie Andrews
6. Veronica Lodge
7. Ashleigh Murray
8. Kevin Keller
9. Betty Cooper
10. Jughead Jones
11. Camila Mendes

QUIZ #2: WHO'S MOST LIKELY TO . . . ?

1. All of them
2. KJ
3. Cole
4. Cami
5. Ashleigh or Casey
6. Lili
7. Madelaine
8. Charles

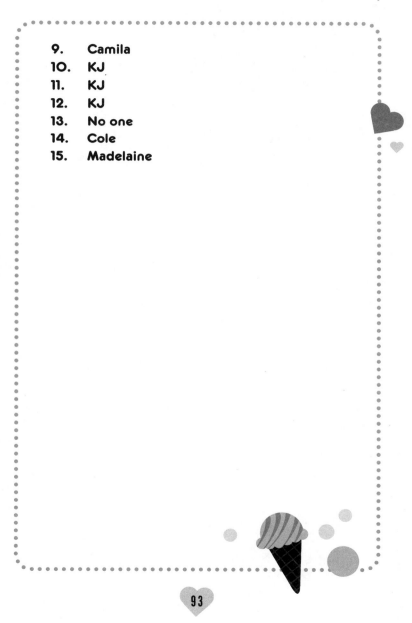

9.   Camila
10.   KJ
11.   KJ
12.   KJ
13.   No one
14.   Cole
15.   Madelaine

HELP US PICK THE
NEXT ISSUE OF

SCOOP!

HERE'S HOW TO VOTE:

Go to

www.ReadScoop.com

**to cast your vote for
who we should
SCOOP! next.**

Cast of Riverdale

Be like the **Cast** of **Riverdale!**

In September 2017, Lili Reinhart posted on Instagram to her millions of followers to show her support as a mental health advocate.

Here's the **SCOOP!** on how *you* can help raise awareness about mental health:

- 💜 **INSPIRE** others to get involved on social media to spread the word.
- 💜 **ENCOURAGE** open communication. Hearing people talk honestly about mental illness may encourage others to seek help.
- 💜 **EDUCATE** others about fighting the stigma attached to mental illness.